Moto X

The Ultimate User Guide

Disclaimer

Contents

Summary of the Report

Hi,

Hope you are doing fine and are ready to benefit from the abundant features offered by your brand new Moto X phone. In this eBook I have given a complete guide for the Moto X phone which will aid in benefitting you so that you can use your phone in a much better way. It includes detailed descriptions about the basics of the phone, and the various other facilitates that the phone has to offer. I have also included the key specifications of the phone at the end of this book, which give you an overall gist of what the phone is about.

If you have just bought this phone or are a new user of this phone, then this user guide can be really beneficial for you, as it will give you an understanding of the phone. I have also included various visual displays in the guide that will help you comprehend the text in the book in a clearer way.

Get to know your Moto X with this user guide so that you can make the most of your smartphone!

Introduction to the Moto X

When it comes to the Moto X, the phone needs no introduction. This amazing android gadget, launched in August of last year is already making its mark in the market. With the sophistication of voice recognition, touching this phone is completely optional. The phone also knows that your time is really important therefore it will give you subtle notifications so that you do not have to constantly check your phone.

This revolutionary phone is the king when it comes to customization because it lets you customize the outer appearance of the phone as you wish. The headphones also come in colors that match the back of your phone thus making the overall phone very appealing. The 10 megapixel camera of the phone makes use of Clear Pixel technology that lets the phone soak much more light.

Moto X aims to make your life easier with features and benefits that will knock your socks off!

How the Phone Looks Like

Below is a picture showing the key external features of the Moto X. you can compare these key features with your own phone so that you can get a better idea as to what each component does. This way, you can be better acquainted with your phone.

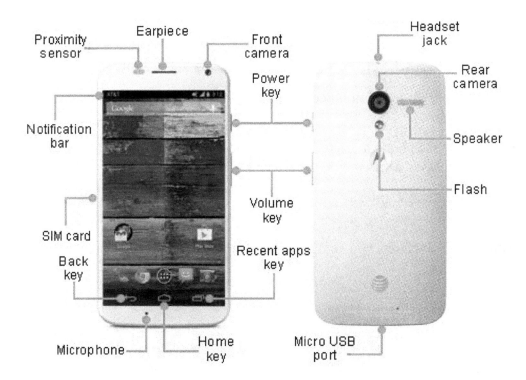

Phone Basics

The Layout

The **Front Camera** of the phone allows for taking pictures and making videos while you face the screen, thus making it easier to carry out certain tasks and video conference.

The **Power Button** is a key feature which lets you turn your phone and the screen on and off. It also helps to switch phone to either vibration, silent or airplane mode.

Volume button helps to increase or decrease the volume of your phone with respect to your ringtone, phone call or when you are viewing certain media applications.

The **Microphone** helps to transmit voice during phone calls or record sounds during making videos or voice recordings.

Flash on the back of the phone helps to illuminate the objects especially in less light while taking a picture or making a video.

Both the **Front and Back Cameras** allow you to take pictures and make videos as and when you like.

Micro USB/charger Jack lets you connect a USB cable or your phone charger to your phone.

Turning Your Phone On and Off

When you turn your phone on, your device might indicate 'Searching for Service', which means that it is waiting for your phone to find signals. Once that is done, your phone will be on standby, and you can start using it.

Turning your phone off would require you to press and hold the power key and then wait for the phone options menu where you simply have to press 'Power off'.

Turning Your Screen On and Off

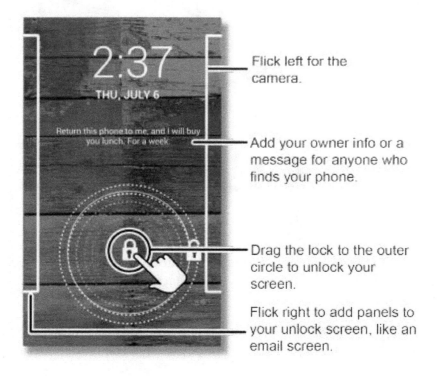

Flick left for the camera.

Add your owner info or a message for anyone who finds your phone.

Drag the lock to the outer circle to unlock your screen.

Flick right to add panels to your unlock screen, like an email screen.

With this phone, you can easily turn the screen off when you are not using the phone and then turn it on and unlock it whenever need be. To turn it off, you need to press the Power key once. When you press your Power key again or in the case that you get a phone call, the phone screen will appear again and the lock screen will show.

The phone, in order to save battery, will automatically turn your screen off after some time of inactivity. While off, you can still receive calls, messages and active notifications.

Adjusting Sound

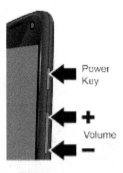

To control or adjust the sound of any current feature that is open on your phone, you can use the volume keys as shown in the above diagram. There are three types of volume control, the ringer volume, earpiece volume and the music/video volume.

Finding Phone Number

You can find your phone number by going to your phone settings and then about phone. In your about phone you will find the status option in which you can see 'my phone number'.

Touchscreen Navigation

You can use various commands on your touchscreen and navigate your phone simply though touching gestures. These gestures let you select icons or drag these icons to various locations. When you have to scroll through messages, contacts or your app list, you can simply do so by the flick of your finger or quick strokes in either horizontal or vertical direction.

Home Screen

Your home screen is your main display screen from where you can start using applications or other functions on the phone. You can also customize your home screen however you like and add apps, widgets or make folders. If you flick your home screen towards the left or right, you can see additional home screen space that is available to you. F you flick down from the top, you will go onto settings and notifications.

You can add apps and other things to your home screen by dragging icons from the app list and releasing it onto the home screen panel. You can make folders of different apps on the home screen but dragging and dropping similar apps onto one another.

To remove apps from the home screen you can simply hold the app and drag it to 'Remove' on top of the screen.

App List

Your phone' app list will show you all of your applications in your phone. You can access your app list from your phone's home screen by touching on the following icon:

You can flick left or right on your app list to see all your apps. If you download a new app from your Google Play Store, the app will be added onto your existing app list.

Recent Apps

The recent apps that you have used can be accessed by using the following icon on your phone:

Search

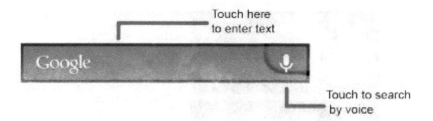

The above Google search widget helps your search for anything online. You can tap on it to begin your search and you will even be getting various suggestions for your search. You can search by text or by voice.

Google Now

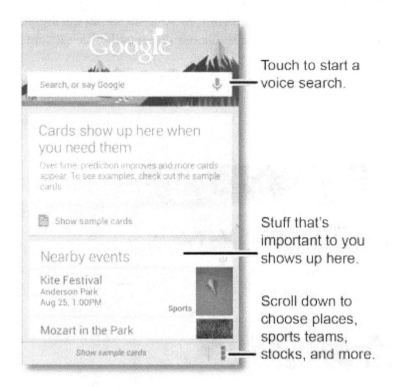

Google Now uses your location, searches, and other Google services to provide you with all the information you might need and when you need it. The great thing about this is, that the service is always working in the background which means that you do not have to do or ask for anything. Whenever new information is available, Google will automatically notify you.

To get started with Google Now, you can touch and hold the home icon and then drag your finger up to the Google Now circle icon. Once your finger reaches there, you can release it.

Motorola Assist

The Motorola Assist helps in assisting you while you are busy with other tasks. So for instance, if you are driving, the assist can respond to messages for you, during meetings it can help silence your ringer and so forth. It gives you a suggestion in your status bat during your day to day activities and all you have to do is flick the status bar down and either accept the status or delete it.

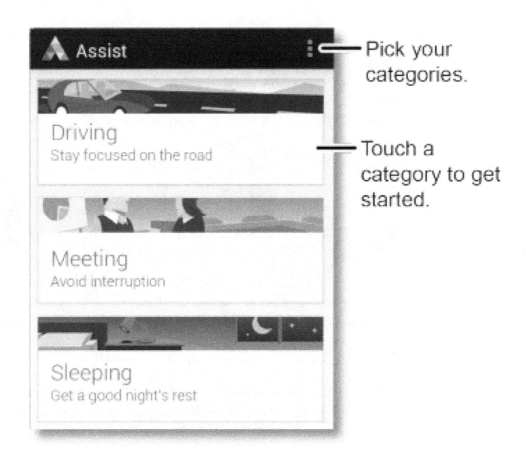

Entering Text

You can enter text through the touchscreen keyboard. There are a lot of keyboard options which make using the keyboard easier for you such as cutting, copying, and pasting, along with continuous key (gesture) input, voice to text input, user dictionary customization predictive text and so much more.

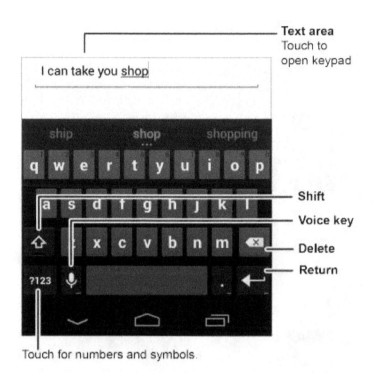

Touchless Voice Control

The touchless voice control helps you to command your phone without having to touch it. But this is not easy as you have to train your phone to be able to recognize your voice. You can access this option by going to settings, and then touchless control within settings.

Voice control helps you with entering text messages or in emails. You can add punctuation marks by saying the name of the punctuation mark you want to add.

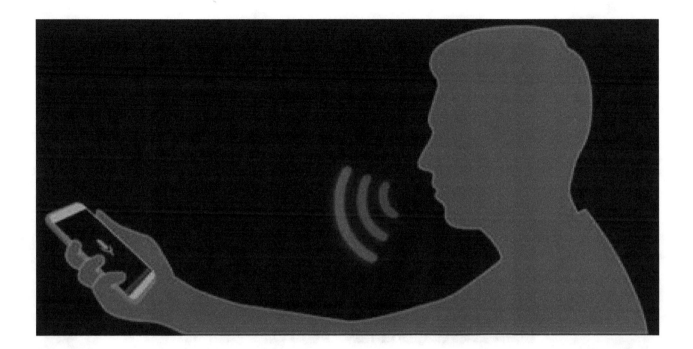

Phone Calling Facilities

Recent Calls & People

Delete numbers you entered.

During a call:

Hang up.

🔍 Find a contact.

📞 Call.

⋮ See options

Phone calls can be made from this phone through several different means i.e. from your dial pad, recently called numbers, or from your contact list. You can even multitask while you are on a call by touching the home icon in order to hide the call display. This way, you can perform other tasks such as look up a phone number or go on other apps. You can come back on your call display by flicking down the status bar and touching 'Ongoing call'.

Contacts

Your contacts application helps you to store contact information of the people around you.

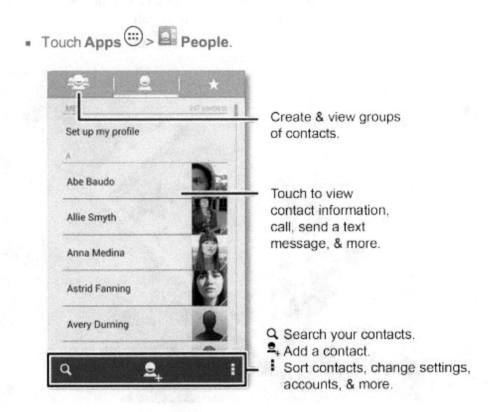

Adding a new contact is really simple. You can either use your phone's people application to add a contact, or you can directly add a contact via your phone dial pad. You can fill in as much or as little information as you require. There are various fields in the phone that you can fill out such as phone numbers, email address, home address and even occupation related information. Once you are finished with this, you can touch the "Done" option on top.

If you want to edit your existing contact database, you can simply go on to the contact list, touch on the contact that you want to make changes to, then touch the three vertical dots on the top right corner of your screen and touch the edit option.

Messaging and Accounts

With your Moto X, you have the opportunity to create various accounts and use its messaging capabilities via Gmail, text messaging, emails, Google Talk and social media networking accounts.

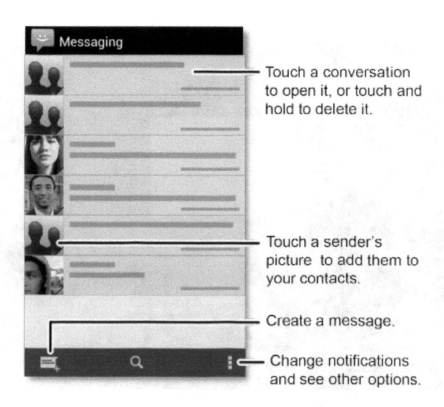

As far as personal text messages go, you can use it to message any other messaging ready or wireless phone. To compose a message you select the messaging icon and then touch the Compose icon to add in a new message. You can send a message to multiple people by separating phone numbers with a comma as and when you insert phone numbers.

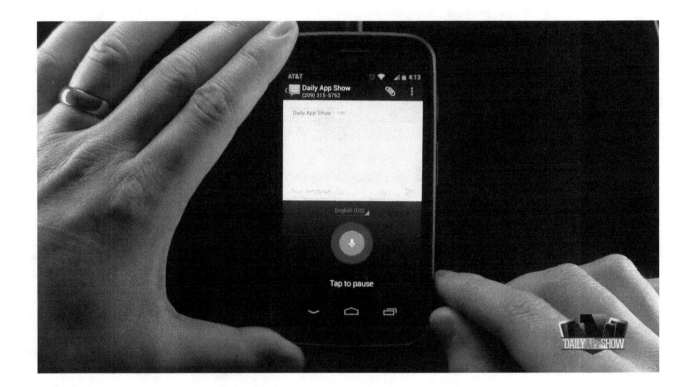

Apps and Entertainment

Your Google Play Store is the place where you will find all the amazing Apps your phone has to offer. You can choose from a wide variety of apps which consist of both paid and free apps. If you want an app, all you have to do is tap on it and hit install. You can find different categories of apps and you even have the option for searching for any specific app that you desire.

If you download an app which you later on want to remove from your phone, you go to the Apps section on your phone, find the App, then press and hold the app until the 'Remove' option comes on the top. After that all you have to do is drag the app to the 'Remove' option.

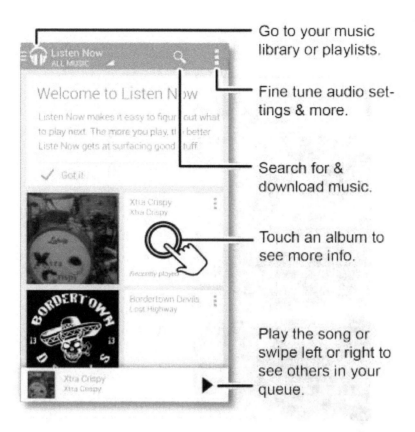

Go to your music
library or playlists.

Fine tune audio set-
tings & more.

Search for &
download music.

Touch an album to
see more info.

Play the song or
swipe left or right to
see others in your
queue.

Google Play lets you experience the world of entertainment firsthand by giving you a platform to enjoy your favorite music, TV shows, movies, books and various apps and games.

Web and Data

Due to your phone's inbuilt technology, you can access the internet via Wi-Fi, Mobile Data Services, 4G and the VPN.

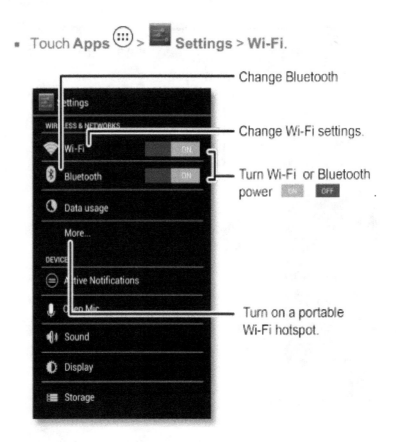

The Wi-Fi option lets you connect to the internet as long as you have access to it. You can click on the Wi-Fi tab and scroll through the options of whatever internet connections are available to you. Turning the Wi-Fi off when not in use can be really beneficial to conserve battery.

Open options.

Show other
browser tabs, or
open a new one.

Touch a link to
select it. Touch &
hold for more
options.

This browser on your phone lets you access the World Wide Web and therefore, you can use
your phone the same way as you would use your laptop. You even have a voice search option
where you can use your voice to search for various topics. This way, you will not have to type.

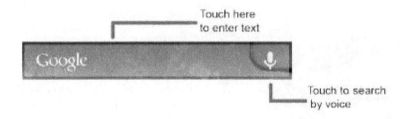

Touch here
to enter text

Touch to search
by voice

Calendar and Tools

The **calendar** app on your phone is great for managing your important tasks such as meetings, events, and appointments.

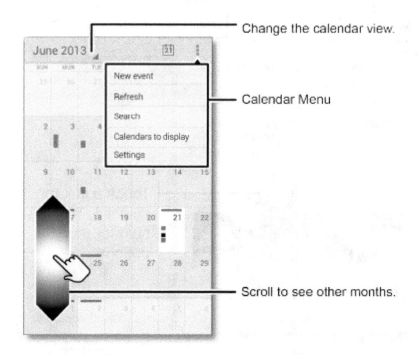

To add new events to your calendar, you can touch the menu button on the top, and then tap on 'Newevent'. You can even set a reminder for this event so that you do not forget about it in any case. Once you are done with creating the event, you can tap on 'Done'.

If you want to make changes to any event, you can simply touch that event and then press on the 'Pen' icon. Tap on 'Done' once you are done. For deleting an event you have to press on the 'Trash' icon. You can even search for specific events in your calendar by using the search facility in your phone.

The **Clock** option in your phone gives you a lot of options with regards to the usage of your clock. You can view the time and set up an alarm for yourself.

The **Calculator** app in your phone lets you make various calculations. You can get access to the calculator by visiting the Apps sections.

You will even find the **Quick office** application in your phone which lets you create or edit presentations, spreadsheets and documents.

You can **Update your phone** by going into settings then system updates and then finally to Update Motorola software.

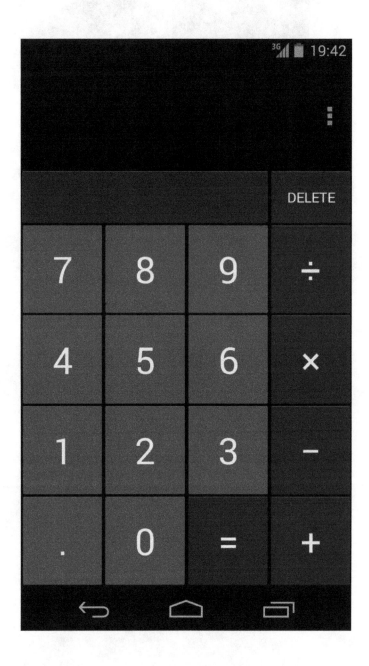

Settings

The settings option includes a lot of things. Here are some of the things that the setting option offers:

Network and Wireless Settings

The settings option consists of Wi-Fi settings, roaming, Bluetooth, wireless network settings and so much more.

The Airplane Mode in your settings option switches off your wireless connections which is useful in the airplane or when you are in an area that does not allow data usage or making calls. Therefore, with this mode, you can use your phone functionalities without making or receiving any calls or accessing online features.

You can turn the Airplane Mode on by pressing and holding the power button and then touching 'Airplane Mode'.

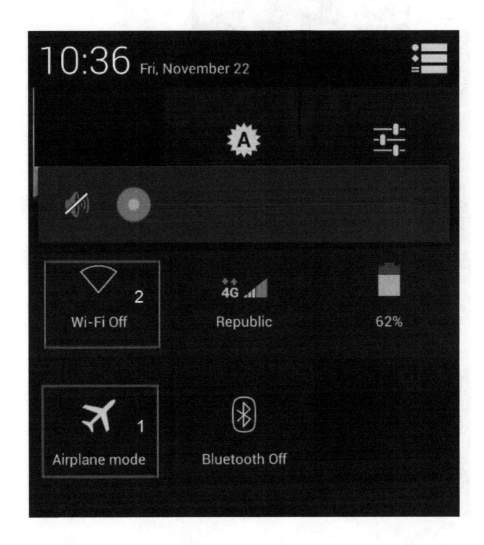

Call Settings

The call settings in your phone allow you to configure voicemail options as well as other call related settings.

For Voicemail settings, you can go to your apps section, then tap on Voicemail, then the menu option and from there you can access settings.

Other Call Settings

Call setting includes options such as dial pad touch tones, voicemail, auto retry, quick responses, Hearing Aids, Voice Privacy, DTMF tones and the TTY mode.

Display Settings

Display setting adjustment of your phone is important for better viewing and to help increase you phone battery life. The display features include brightness of the phone, auto rotate screen, display timeout delay and wallpaper settings. All of this can be adjusted by going on your settings and then pressing the 'Display' option.

Storage Settings

Storage settings allow you to manage the internal storage of your phone. If you want to view how much storage the various applications have consumed, then you can go to your settings option and click on storage. The bars that you will see at the bottom lets you view how much space for storage is left for each app.

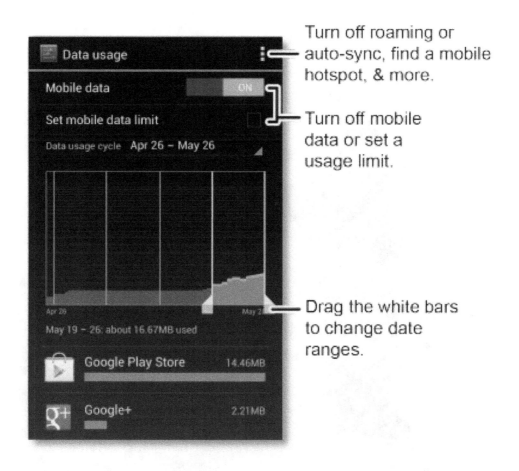

Turn off roaming or auto-sync, find a mobile hotspot, & more.

Turn off mobile data or set a usage limit.

Drag the white bars to change date ranges.

Battery Settings

You can monitor the usage of your phone's battery by going through your settings menu. From there you can see which functions of your phone are consuming what amount of your battery.

The best battery feature in your phone is that it can recharge the battery before becoming fully drained out. You can view this option by going to your apps and the selecting Assist.

Keeping track of your battery is really important so that it doesn't automatically turn off. This can cause loss of important data. You should always use an authentic Motorola charger to charge your phone.

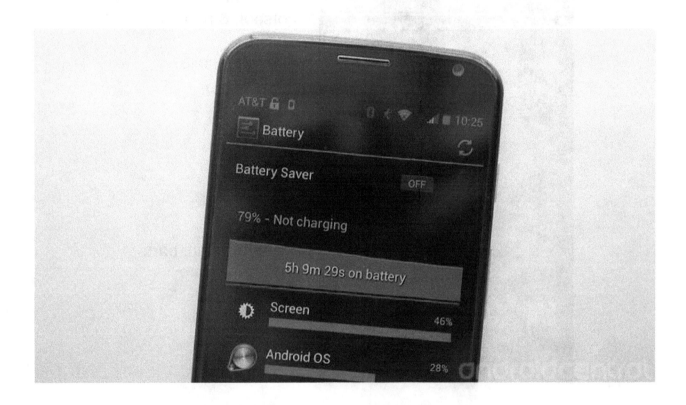

Key Specifications

The Motorola Moto X has the following key specifications:

General Specifications

Released in August of 2013

Dimensions (mm) 129.30 x 65.30 x 10.40

No removable battery

Weight (g) 130.00

Display

Capacitive touchscreen type

Resolution 720x1280 pixels

Screen Size (inches) 4.70

Hardware

RAM 2GB

Processor 1.7GHz dual-core

Processors make Qualcomm MSM8960Pro Snapdragon

16GB of internal Storage

Software

No java support or browser supporting flash

Operating system Android 4.2

Camera

Flash yes

Rear camera 10 megapixel

Front camera 2 megapixel

Connectivity

Wi-Fi yes

GPS Yes

Bluetooth Yes, v 4.00

Headphones 3.5mm

Number of SIMs 1

Micro USB

Charging via micro USB yes

Nano SIM type

Sensors

No temperature Sensor

Barometer

Gyroscope

Compass/Magnetometer

Accelerometer

Proximity sensor

No ambient light sensor

Conclusion

The Moto X phone is a powerful device to have at one's disposal. Whether you like to take multiple pictures a day or love to use different apps, this Android powered beast will exceed your expectations and then some. The picture illustrations in this book have been put in so that you can better understand the various features of the phone.

We hope that you found this guide to be more than helpful, and now know your Moto X inside out. Feel free to contact us if you have any queries or want to share your thoughts about this guide.

www.ingramcontent.com/pod-product-compliance
Lightning Source LLC
Chambersburg PA
CBHW060509060326
40689CB00020B/4691